4/98

Jaguars

By Michael Green

Reading Consultant:
Karen Miller

CAPSTONE PRESS

MANKATO, MINNESOTA

C A P S T O N E   P R E S S
818 North Willow Street • Mankato, MN 56001

Printed in the United States of America.

Library of Congress Cataloging-in-Publication Data
Green, Michael (Michael R.)
    Jaguars/by Michael Green.
    p. cm. -- (High performance)
    Includes bibliographical references and index.
    Summary: Gives an overview of the history of the stylish Jaguar, describing some notable models.
    ISBN 1-56065-393-0
    1. Jaguar automobile--Juvenile literature. [1. Jaguar automobile--History.] I. Title. II. Series: High performance (Mankato, Minn.)
TL215.J3G74 1996
629.22'2--dc20

                              96-27763
                              CIP
                              AC

Photo credits
Dennis Adler, cover. Behring Automobile Museum, 12-17. FPG/Thomas Craig, 47; Nicolay Zurek, 34 Jaguar Cars Archives, 6-11, 19-25, 28-33, 36, 41. Karen Miller, 26.Unicorn/Kathy Hamer, 4; Aneal Vohra, 38.

Table of Contents

Words in **boldface** type in the text are defined in the Glossary in the back of this book.

Chapter 1

Jaguars

The Jaguar name does not represent any one car. It is the name of an English company that has built classy and beautiful cars since the early 1900s.

The Englishman who made Jaguar famous was Sir William Lyons. His genius as a body stylist made people notice Jaguars wherever they went.

Jaguars are known for their powerful engines and wonderful handling. Jaguar racing cars have won races around the world. Many car buyers want to own a vehicle that is part of the Jaguar tradition.

Through the years, the Jaguar name has appeared on everything from sharp-looking sports cars to fancy luxury **sedans**. The common feature that unites all Jaguar cars is their **flair**.

The Jaguar name has appeared on everything from sports cars to sedans.

Chapter 2

Jaguar's Beginnings

William Lyons was a motorcycle buff. In 1920, Lyons and a partner, William Walmsley, began building motorcycle **sidecars**. Lyons and Walmsley named their new business the Swallow Sidecar Company.

By 1926, Lyons and his partner began applying their talents to building custom automobile bodies. The **frames** and engines for their cars came from other builders. They changed the company's name to the Swallow Sidecar and Coachbuilding Company.

The Swallow Sidecar Company was run by WIlliam Lyons before he started making Jaguar cars.

Lyons and his partner soon became frustrated fitting their car bodies on other designers' frames. They settled on a frame design they liked. They asked the Standard Motor Company to build it. The Standard Motor Company also provided the engines for these new cars.

The First Jaguars

Lyons' first cars were the S.S. I and S.S. II. The S.S.s were shown to the public in 1931 at

The S.S. I coupe was first shown to the public in 1931.

the London Motor Show. The S.S. II was a smaller version of the S.S. I.

Both cars caused a sensation. Their bodies were low to the ground. Their hoods were very long. The long, low, sporty look was popular with the car-buying public.

In 1933, Lyons introduced the S.S. I Tourer. It had an open top. The regular S.S. I and S.S. II had enclosed tops. The Tourer was entered into a car race and won. A smaller S.S. II Tourer was also introduced.

Prewar Jaguars (1935-1938)

The 1936 sedan model was the first Lyons-built car to use the Jaguar name. Legend has it that Lyons had 500 animal names to choose from. He chose the Jaguar name because it represented power, speed, and courage.

Another 1936 model was called the S.S. Jaguar 100. It was an open-topped sports car. With these vehicles, Lyons fulfilled his ambition to build cars entirely of his own design.

During World War II (1939-1945), Jaguar survived by building military aircraft. Jaguar built the famous Spitfire fighter plane and many bombers. To help the war effort, Jaguar built many aircraft parts. Jaguar also built motorcycle sidecars for military use.

After the war, the company officially became Jaguar Cars Limited. Jaguar was

The 1936 S.S. Jaguar 100 was one of the first cars to use the Jaguar name.

committed to building popular cars that offered excellent value for the money.

Chapter 3

Postwar Jaguars

With their postwar vehicles, Jaguar dropped the S.S. label. Most of the company's cars were given the initials XK and a model number.

The XK was the name of the engine that powered the car. X meant experimental. K was the alphabetical character of the final engine model selected for production. This basic engine was so successful that versions of it remained in Jaguars until the mid-1980s.

The XK 150 was one of the first Jaguars to use the legendary XK engine.

The XK 120 Roadster

Lyons developed a powerful car engine that produced 160 **horsepower**. He decided to design a new sports car body to go along with it. Then both the car's styling and performance would attract public attention.

Lyons' new sports car appeared in 1948. It was known as the Jaguar XK 120 Roadster. The XK 120 was destined to become one of the greatest sports cars of all time.

The name XK 120 was based on the car's top speed of 120 miles (192 kilometers) per hour. This made it one of the fastest **production cars** in the world. Many orders for the new XK 120 flooded into Lyons' factory.

In 1950, Lyons entered his XK 120 in the world-famous 24-hour race at Le Mans in France. The XK 120 did not finish in the top three positions. Lyons decided to build a version of the XK 120 especially for racing.

Racing the Jaguar

Le Mans is a French race course made up of local highways. The Le Mans course has

The XK 120 was one of the greatest sports cars ever.

excellent road surfaces. There are long straightaways and difficult, fast corners.

Each car at Le Mans must have at least two drivers. The drivers take turns driving the same car for 24 hours straight. Le Mans cars must be fast and reliable. To win at Le Mans, a car must handle well and have excellent brakes.

To build a racing version of the XK 120 sports car, the engineers at Jaguar decided to reduce the car's weight. The all-steel frame was replaced by a lightweight, **multi-tubular frame**.

The new body was made of **aluminum**. It was designed by a former airplane engineer to be as **aerodynamic** as possible.

C-Type Jaguars

The racing Jaguar used the same engine as the production XK 120. The racing car became known as the XK 120C or the C-type.

Three of the C-types were finished in time to enter the 1951 Le Mans race. One of them won. The other two had mechanical problems that took them out of the race.

Jaguar's XK 120, shown above, was also made into a race car called the C-type.

At Le Mans, the C-type Jaguar beat older, better-known cars. Jaguar sales increased dramatically. Jaguar was finally recognized as a leading European carmaker.

Jaguar Popularity

For a time, Jaguars became the most popular foreign car in the United States. Such famous movie stars as Clark Gable, Spencer Tracy, Humphrey Bogart, and Cary Grant became proud Jaguar owners.

Jaguars were popular around the world because they were fast, easy to drive, and stunningly beautiful. Jaguars were also more affordable than other sports cars.

Improved Jaguars

In 1953, Jaguar improved the XK 120 C-type racer. The improved Jaguar was fitted with **disc brakes** instead of **drum brakes**. Other race cars still used the drum brakes. With the better disc brakes, Jaguar race cars finished first, second, and fourth at Le Mans.

There was an ever-growing demand for Jaguars, especially in the United States. So Lyons came out with the XK 140. It was based on the XK 120, though the engine was modified and the steering was improved.

Many famous movie stars in the United States owned XK 120s.

Nearly 9,000 XK 140s were built between 1954 and 1957. Most of these cars were shipped to the United States.

Chapter 4

Jaguar Racing Cars

In 1954, Jaguar came out with a new racing car. It was designed to compete at Le Mans. It was known as the D-type. It was very different from the C-type. It no longer had a frame.

Instead, the D-type depended on the strength of its body **panels** to hold it together. The front end of the car was bolted to the center section. The front end supported both the engine and the front **suspension**. The rear section of the car housed the gas tank and the spare wheel. The rear section was also bolted onto the center section.

The Jaguar D-type was a new design. Its body panels held it together.

The XK-SS was a road version of the D-type racer.

To improve the speed of the D-type, the XK engine was modified to produce 250 horsepower. A new type of **lubrication system** allowed the hood to be lowered. This new hood style lowered the car's center of gravity. A low center of gravity allowed the car to hug the road at high speeds.

From 1954 to 1956, a total of 42 D-type racing Jaguars were made. In its time, the D-type was one of the world's most famous race cars.

In response to public demand, Jaguar developed the XK-SS. It was a road version of the D-type racer. Only 16 were built before a fire destroyed all the machines needed to make any more of the XK-SSs.

A New Generation of Jaguars

In 1957, Jaguar began building the XK 150 in both open-topped and hardtopped versions. The XK 150 was an upgraded version of the XK 140. The XK 150 was the first production car with disc brakes.

By the late 1950s, Lyons and his top engineers started to think about developing a new sports car for the public. They wanted to use features developed for the D-type racing Jaguars.

The Jaguar XK-E

The fruit of their labor was the E-type. In the United States, it was popularly called the XK-E. The E-type came off the Jaguar **production line** in 1961. It was a replacement for the aging XK 150.

The XK-E came in both open-top and hardtop versions. They were very fast. They had incredible acceleration, great handling, and good looks.

In 1965, Jaguar introduced a more powerful engine for the XK-E. It came with an automatic **transmission**. The XK-E sports car was sold in more than 34 countries. It was a major moneymaker for many years.

Improving the XK-E

The next major change to the XK-E series occurred in 1971. It was given a very powerful **V-12** engine. With this engine, the car became known as the Series III E-type.

The new engine could push the Series III E-type car up to 150 miles (240 kilometers) per hour. Due to its growing size and weight, the Series III E-type could not really be considered a sports car anymore. It had become a fancy touring car.

The XK-E has been out of production since 1975. Still, it is often the model people

The Jaguar E-type was often called the XK-E.

instantly associate with Jaguar. About 73,000
XK-E Jaguars were built over a 13-year period.

Chapter 5
Jaguar Sedans

Jaguar builds more than just sports cars. Jaguar has a long history of building fast and beautiful sedans. The medium-sized Jaguar sedans have always sold well. Between 1955 and 1967, Jaguar sold about 121,000 medium-sized sedans.

In 1967, the Jaguar Mark 2 medium-sized sedan was offered in two economical versions, the 240 or 340 sedan. The 340 had a bigger engine than the 240. The 240 and 340 sedans were affordable cars. They were made for people who could not afford top-of-the-line Jaguar models.

The Mark 2 was Jaguar's best-selling sedan for many years.

About 19,000 Mark Xs were built from 1961 through 1966.

The largest sedan in the Jaguar lineup was the XK-powered Mark VII. This car was followed in 1956 by the Mark VIII luxury sedan. The Mark VIII had an improved XK engine producing 210 horsepower.

In 1958, the Mark VIII was replaced by the Mark IX. The Mark X replaced the Mark IX in

1961. About 19,000 Mark Xs were built until the car's name was changed in 1966. The Mark X became the 420 G. About 6,000 420 Gs were built until production stopped in 1970.

The Jaguar XJ6

In 1968, Jaguar began producing a four-seat, hardtop, luxury sedan known as the XJ6. The XJ6 replaced all of Jaguar's earlier sedans.

The original XJ6 was considered one of the world's best luxury cars. It was replaced in 1974 by an improved model known as the Series II XJ6. The Series II XJ6 remained in production until 1979. The Series II XJ6 was replaced by the Series III XJ6 in 1979.

In 1986, Jaguar developed a brand new car to carry on the XJ6 name. Some members of the press call this car the XJ 40. This helped distinguish the new Jaguar from the rest of the XJ6 series.

The number XJ 40 was the car's internal product code number at Jaguar. The XJ 40 had an aluminum engine, replacing the XK's original steel engine.

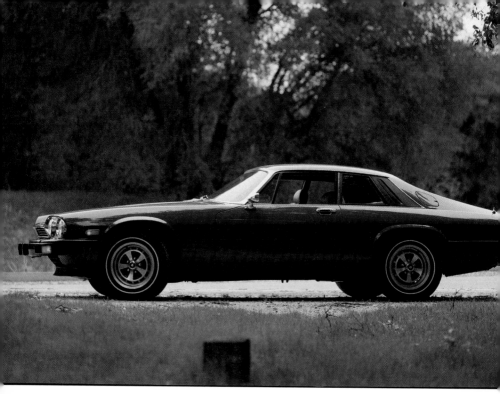

The XJS was introduced in 1975.

In 1994, Jaguar gave the XJ6 a new body style. This version of the XJ6 series is often called the X 300.

The X330 Jaguar

In 1996, Jaguar introduced the extended-wheelbase XJ6. The vehicle's code name was the X330. The X330 comes in two model types, the XJ12 and the Vanden Plas.

The X330 comes with either a six-cylinder engine or a larger V-12 engine. The V-12 is in the XJ12 version. Both models are five inches longer than the standard XJ6.

The Original XJ12

The original XJ12 was first made in late 1972. Unfortunately, the XJ12 rolled out of the Jaguar factory just as a worldwide oil crisis hit. Sales of the new XJ12 slumped so badly that Jaguar stopped production of the vehicle in 1977.

With a new and more powerful V-12 engine, the XJ12 was reintroduced in 1994. Top speed was about 140 miles (224 kilometers) per hour. It went from zero to 60 miles (96 kilometers) per hour in 7.3 seconds.

XJS Jaguar

In 1975, the Jaguar XJS **coupe**, a two-seater, was introduced. The XJS had a top speed of 153 miles (245 kilometers) per hour. From a standing start, it could reach 100 miles (160 kilometers) per hour in 16.9 seconds.

The XJS was a coupe built on a shortened and modified XJ6 frame. It was originally offered only with the V-12 engine. Beginning in 1993, the XJS was also available with a six-cylinder engine.

Responding to popular demand, Jaguar introduced an open-topped version of the XJS in 1985. The car was not a **convertible** in the usual sense of the word. The roof consisted of removable panels that were stowed in the trunk until needed. A true convertible version of the XJS with a power-operated roof was introduced in 1988.

The End of the XJ6

Since its introduction in the early 1970s, more than 100,000 Jaguar XJS coupes and convertibles have been built. Production of the XJS series ended in 1996. The car is already considered a classic by many collectors. When XJSs appear in car dealers' showrooms, they are snapped up by buyers.

The XJS convertible was last made in 1996.

The last XJS convertible had an aluminum AJ 16 engine. It had **alloy** wheels. The steering wheel and shift knob were made of matching wood and leather. A jaguar cat is embossed on the head restraints.

Chapter 6

Safety and the Future

Modern Jaguar cars have many of today's best safety features. These include seat belts, air bags, safety glass and crash-resistant bumpers.

Jaguars, like most modern cars, are designed with bodies that crumple upon impact. This allows the front and rear sections of the car to absorb most of the impact during a crash.

The sides of cars are too thin to crumple without harming a vehicle's occupant. So

Steel bars in the doors of Jaguars protect passengers.

The 1997 Jaguar XK8

Jaguar has provided steel reinforcement bars inside car doors.

To prevent car doors from popping open in an accident, Jaguar cars have anti-burst locks. These locks secure the door to the vehicle's door frame for added protection.

If a Jaguar is struck from behind, the occupants are protected from whiplash by both their seat belts and built-in headrests.

The Future of Jaguar

In 1997, the XJS series was replaced by a new series of Jaguar cars known as the XK 8. The XK8 is the future of Jaguar. It was first shown to the public at car shows in Geneva and New York City early in 1996.

The XK8 is available in coupe and convertible models. It has a newly-designed V-8 engine called the AJ-V8. Like the classic Jaguars, the interior is leather with wood trim.

A Change in Ownership

Sir William Lyons retired from his company in 1972. Until the end of his 50-year career,

Jaguar displays the latest safety features at car shows.

Lyons continued to direct improvements and styling changes that brought Jaguar worldwide success in selling cars. He died in 1985. In 1966, Jaguar merged with the British Motor Corporation. The new company was called British Motor Holdings.

British Motor Holdings merged with Leyland Motors in 1968. The new company was called British Leyland Motors. Besides selling Jaguars, British Leyland sold other British cars including MG, Triumph, Rover, and Austin. British Leyland was taken over by the British government in the mid-1970s.

Jaguar became an independent company again in 1984. Ford Motor Company bought Jaguar in 1989. Under the control of the Ford Motor Company, Jaguars are still built in England. The Jaguar tradition of class and quality continues today.

From 1968 until the mid-1970s, Jaguar was part of the British Leyland group of carmakers.

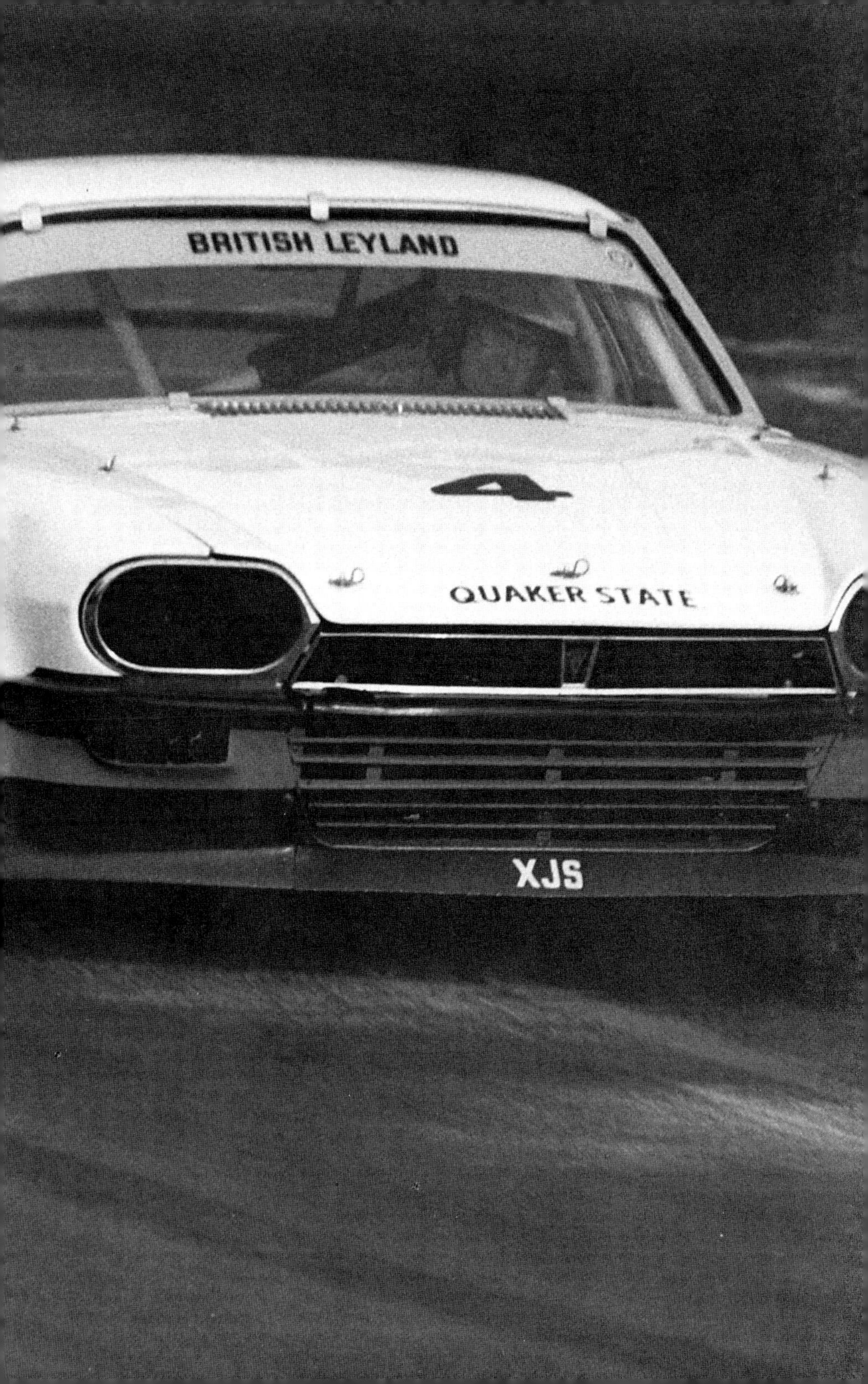
BRITISH LEYLAND
4
QUAKER STATE
XJS

Glossary

aerodynamic—designed to cut down on wind resistance

alloy—two or more metals fused for extra strength

aluminum—a strong, lightweight metal

concept car—vehicle built to show off an idea

convertible—a car with a soft fabric top that can be raised or lowered

coupe—two-door hardtop car

disc brakes—an efficient type of brake that works by causing two pads to press on either side of a disc that rotates with the wheel

drum brakes—a type of brake that works by causing two pads to press against only one side of a drum that rotates with the wheel. Drum brakes are less efficient than disc brakes.

flair—something that is especially striking and stylish

frame—skeletal structure around which a car is built

horsepower—a unit used to measure the power of engines and motors

lubrication system—parts in an engine that keep a constant bath of oil on high-friction areas

mid-engined car—a car designed with the engine in the middle of the car rather than in the front or back to get a low center of gravity

multi-tubular frame—a lightweight frame made of hollow metal pipes welded together

panels—parts that make up the body of a car

production cars—cars made for sale to the public

production line—a system of work stations inside a factory

sedans—hardtop cars with two or four doors and a front and rear seat

sidecars—a small car attached to the side of a motorcycle for carrying a passenger

suspension—a set of springs and shocks connecting a car's wheels to its body

transmission—one of the devices that transfers the engine's power to the wheels

V-12—an engine with twelve cylinders set in pairs at angles forming the shape of the letter V

To Learn More

Barris, George. *Famous Custom and Show Cars*. New York: E.P. Dutton, 1973.

Martin, John. *The World's Most Exotic Cars*. Minneapolis: Capstone Press, 1994.

Nicholson, T.R. *Sports Cars*. New York: Macmillan, 1969.

Stephenson, Sallie. *Sports Cars*. Mankato, Minn.: Capstone Press, 1991.

Useful Addresses

The Behring Auto Museum
3750 Blackhawk Plaza Circle
Danville, CA 94506

Jaguar Cars Archives
555 MacArthur Boulevard
Mahwah, NJ 07430-2327

Jaguar Clubs of North America
9685 McLeod Road
Chilliwack, BC V2P 6H4
Canada

National Automobile Museum
10 Lake Street South
Reno, NV 89501

Welsh Classics Car Museum
P.O. Box 4130
Steubenville, OH 43952

Internet Sites

JagWeb
http://www.oslonett.no/home/nick/jaguar.html

Welsh Jaguar Classic Car Museum
http://www.classicar.com/museums/
welshjag/welshjag.htm

Jaguar Drivers' Club
http://huizen.dds.nl/~jdc/

Jaguar Association of New England
http://users.aol.com/ajowens/jane.htm

The Jaguar hood ornament reminds people of
power and style.

Index